The Mythology of the Trojan War: The History and Legacy of the Mythical Legends about the Battle for Troy

By Charles River Editors

A painting depicting Achilles

About Charles River Editors

Charles River Editors is a boutique digital publishing company, specializing in bringing history back to life with educational and engaging books on a wide range of topics. Keep up to date with our new and free offerings with this 5 second sign up on our weekly mailing list, and visit Our Kindle Author Page to see other recently published Kindle titles.

We make these books for you and always want to know our readers' opinions, so we encourage you to leave reviews and look forward to publishing new and exciting titles each week.

Introduction

Achilles and the Nereid Cymothoe: Attic red-figure kantharos from Volci (Cabinet des Médailles, Bibliothèque nationale, Paris)

The Mythology of the Trojan War

"Like leaves on trees the race of man is found, —

Now green in youth, now withering on the ground;

Another race the following spring supplies:

They fall successive, and successive rise." – *The Iliad*

Perhaps the most famous epic poems ever written, the *Iliad* and the *Odyssey* have been read for nearly 3,000 years, making them some of the oldest written works in the Western world. The poems made characters like Paris, Helen, Odysseus, Achilles, Hector, and Ajax instantly recognizable, and they also influenced other ancient poets like Virgil, whose *Aeneid* is clearly modeled after them. The epic poems also literally put Troy on the map, motivating Heinrich Schliemann to search for and ultimately find the city of Troy in the 19th century.

Believed to be penned around the 8th century BCE or 7th century BCE, the *Iliad* and the *Odyssey* served as both entertainment and a moral guidebook of sorts for the ancient Greeks, as well as the foundation for Western literature. Although there is some scholarly debate regarding the epic's authorship, it is generally attributed to Homer. Given that he lived nearly 2800 years ago, not much is actually known about Homer; even his birthplace is debated, but due to the dialect of Greek in which the works attributed to him were written, it is generally believed that he lived in Iona. The only other aspect of Homer's life that is generally agreed upon is that he was a blind poet, possibly also a bard. That naturally raises the question of how he wrote his epic poetry, but scholars assume he probably dictated them to a scribe, as the format suggests they were comprised from various shorter forms of oral poetry.

Even people who don't know much about ancient Greek mythology can probably still name Achilles, the Trojan Horse, and a number of other gods that play a part in the story of the Trojan War. The enduring nature of this story led to many great people claiming descent from one of the characters found within it; for example, Alexander the Great was said to have slept with a copy of Homer's *Iliad* every night during his campaigns, a description of the legendary war that describes the epitome of pre-hoplite warfare and is still taught at military academies around the world today. The entire story, from its fickle beginnings to its catastrophic end, has made its way to modern readers via surviving sources which, when combined, form a biopsy of ancient Greek myth and many of its finest elements.

Most people could be forgiven for mistakenly believing that the *Iliad* encompasses the entire story of the Trojan War, but the *Iliad* tells the story of just four days in the ninth year of the war. In many ways, the *Iliad* is the story of "Achilles's wrath," which actually serves as a subtitle in some editions, but in order to gain an idea of the full story of what occurred at Troy between ancient heroes Achilles, Hector, Menelaus, and Paris, among others, readers must collate sources (often fragmentary) stretching from the 8th century BCE to Roman sources in the 1st century CE. Indeed, piecing the story together is one of the intentions of this epic poem.

Another intention of the *Iliad* is to highlight the nature of the story as a work of mythology — not history. Although there are certainly historical elements in the story, as well as certain seminal moments that affected cult activity in ancient Greece, emphasis is placed on the narrative methods that make it an enduring and iconic mixture of myth, legend, and folklore.

Since the story of the Trojan War permeates so many of the ancient myths recounted in literature and theater from the Archaic Period onward, it is always important to understand that the Trojan War itself was a nexus in ancient Greek mythological thought. It was referenced by countless writers in the ancient world because it is the preeminent story in which the gods' characters emerge in all their fickle, vengeful, and partisan glory. In no other works are the interactions between the gods and their subservient mortals so colorful and extensive. There is a reason, however, why the entire story is so rarely collected; the incredibly expansive nature of the story means that its tendrils follow characters from their Mycenaean centers of power through the curses and prophesies of countless heroes and eponymous founder myths.

The Mythology of the Trojan War: The History and Legacy of the Mythical Legends about the Battle for Troy analyzes the famous myths surrounding one of the most famous wars in history, as well as their origins and the historical grounding for them. Along with pictures depicting important people, places, and events, you will learn about the mythology of the Trojan War like never before.

The Seeds of Strife

Zeus, Lord of the Olympian Gods, son of the Titan Chronos, and third generation of celestial beings to inhabit the cosmos, was restless. His battles with his father's kin for supremacy in the cosmos permitted him to create a race of mortals hitherto unequalled for their intellect and industriousness, and he desired a theatre in which the best of mankind could prove their mettle.

Bellicose and capricious, Zeus soon found an opportunity to test his favorite creation while simultaneously curtailing his own demise. His father Chronos had eaten all of his children to prevent the fulfillment of a prophecy in which one of them would overthrow him, but Zeus was cunning enough to avoid being eaten and brought the prophecy to fruition. Of course, Zeus was not inclined to permit the same thing to happen to him. Upon hearing that one of his own children to Metis would overthrow him, he swallowed her whole while she was pregnant so the children would not be born to Metis but to him. However, a second prophecy of his doom emerged concerning a child of the new object of his lust: the sea nymph Thetis.

Zeus was not normally one to let a prophecy interrupt his amorous intentions, but in the case of Thetis, he decided to abstain from his usual carefulness and instead chose to marry her to the aged King Peleus of Aegina. Zeus orchestrated a great wedding for the couple on Aegina and invited all of the gods — all, that is, except Eris, the goddess of strife and discord.

Zeus's eye then landed upon the city of Sparta and the queen who lived there. Queen Leda was noted for her beauty and her kindness, so Zeus came down from Olympus to her in the guise of a swan fleeing a deadly eagle. Leda was besotted with the divine beauty of this swan and eventually lay with it, consummating Zeus's lust. Soon enough, Leda gave birth to two eggs. Since she had slept with her husband the same night she lay with the swan, there was no way of knowing which egg contained the divine or mortal offspring; nevertheless, when two brothers and two sisters hatched, Leda and Tyndareus adopted them all happily. Kastor and Polydeuces, together known as the *Dioskouroi*, were the brothers born to Leda, and their exploits eventually afforded them a place in the heavens. However, it was their sister, Helen, often said to be the most beautiful woman in the world, who fueled the mythology of the Trojan War.

An ancient depiction of Menelaus and Helen

When Helen matured, the greatest heroes in Greece traveled to Sparta to seek her hand from King Tyndareus. Kings and princes alike vied for her affections and that of her father's, who ultimately had the final decision. However, King Tyndareus took no pride or satisfaction in the attention his daughter received from these men; in fact, he was horrified by it.

Among all men, these kings, princes, and heroes were most easily offended and most likely to group together and lay siege to a city based on their dissatisfaction with the results of the pursuit for Helen's hand. Great heroes, such as Ajax, Diomedes, Menestheus, and cunning Odysseus, occupied the king's court and grew increasingly restless during his indecision. Odysseus, though undoubtedly attracted to Helen, found himself more attracted to the beauty and intelligence of Penelope, daughter of Icarius. Knowing the danger Sparta was in, Odysseus approached King Tyndareus and offered him a solution: if Tyndareus would support him in his suit for Penelope, Odysseus would obtain the vow of all Helen's suitors to accept Tyndareus's decision without bloodshed and defend the marriage of Helen to whomever her father chose. Seeing the wisdom Odysseus would become famous for, Tyndareus accepted his offer.

A Roman bust depicting Odysseus

Menelaus, brother of King Agamemnon of Mycenae, and a great prince in his own right, was less forthcoming in his affections for the Spartan princess. Thus, he asked his brother to go to Sparta in his stead and compete for Helen's hand for him, promising a sacrifice of a hundred oxen to Aphrodite if he were to win Helen's hand.

When the time came to make a decision, Tyndareus named the absent prince Menelaus. Once the news reached Mycenae, Menelaus travelled to Sparta immediately to marry the beautiful Helen. Tyndareus's days were now numbered and soon Menelaus would ascend to the throne of Sparta with his new wife by his side.

However, in the tumult of his successes, Menelaus made the gravest mistake of his life: he forgot the promise he made to Aphrodite. In fact, Zeus had depended on this mistake. At the same time, Eris, ignorant of Zeus's machinations, took great offense at being overlooked by the gods in their celebrations. Before marching to the wedding to confront Zeus on the matter, she first crafted a gift of discord for her fellow immortals, a present designed to punish and remind all of her name. When she arrived, she was stopped at the doors to the great wedding hall by the messenger god Hermes, who told her that Zeus had ordered him not to allow her to enter under any circumstances. Eris did not contest the issue with Hermes but instead let fall a golden apple from her hand and walked away. The apple rolled past Hermes into the hall where the wedding was taking place and found its way into the space between the goddesses Hera, Athena, and Aphrodite.

The apple gleamed from the floor and caught the attention of everybody at the wedding. Inscribed on its skin was "For The Finest," and the three goddesses, equal in beauty and vanity, each claimed it was for her. A great argument ensued between the three, who were capable of tearing the world asunder in their pride. Zeus stepped between his wife and daughters and told them he knew of an impartial mortal who had proven himself worthy of being a fair judge in the past and could ensure a peaceful resolution to their problem.

As a result, Hermes led the three goddesses to the isle of Ida, where a young herdsman named Paris lived. Paris had been exiled from the royal house of Troy after a prophecy had decreed that he would be the downfall of the city if he remained. "The first son born to [Hecuba] was Hector; and when a second babe was about to be born Hecuba dreamed she had brought forth a firebrand, and that the fire spread over the whole city and burned it. When Priam learned of the dream from Hecuba, he sent for his son Aesacus, for he was an interpreter of dreams, having been taught by his mother's father Merops. He declared that the child was begotten to be the ruin of his country and advised that the babe should be exposed."[1]

---

[1] Apollodorus *Biblioteca* 3.12.5

An ancient Roman statue depicting Paris

Once the goddesses arrived, they bathed in the River Ida and presented themselves to Paris in all of their magnificent, naked beauty. Paris, defeated by the divine beauty of all three goddesses, declared that he simply could not choose between them. Deterred but not defeated, the three divine beings approached the young man and began offering him prizes beyond his most ambitious dreams. Hera approached Paris and offered him political power and control over all of Europe and Asia. Athena then strode up to Paris and told him she would offer him wisdom, skill in battle, and the abilities of the greatest warriors living and dead. Then Aphrodite, lithe and sensual as an asp, moved close to Paris and whispered in his ear: "If you present the apple to me, I will give you the love of the most beautiful woman in the world."

Enrique Simonet's "The Judgment of Paris"

Paris had heard of Helen, as most Achaeans and non-Achaeans had, and he knew as well as Aphrodite that she was married to Menelaus. Nevertheless, Paris trusted the goddess of love to fulfill her promise, and he placed the golden apple in her hand. Zeus smiled down on Aphrodite as she exacted her vengeance on Menelaus, aware that thousands would suffer the wrath of Hera and Athena before long.

Meanwhile, back in the royal palace of Sparta, Menelaus enjoyed his newfound position as king and husband to the most beautiful woman in the world. He reveled as only a king ignorant of his wrongdoings could. When news reached him that a young Trojan had arrived in his port, he invited the stranger to dine with him at the palace. "For nine days he was entertained by Menelaus; but on the tenth day, Menelaus having gone on a journey to Crete to perform the obsequies of his mother's father Catreus, (Paris) persuaded Helen to go off with him."[2]

---

[2] Apollodorus *Epitome* E 3.3

Many accuse Helen of capriciousness or even harlotry, but the discerning slave or servant in Menelaus's hall the night Paris entered may have noticed the sound of Eros's bowstring as he shot Helen through the heart on Aphrodite's orders. For his part, Paris was young and rash and foolishly believed that the divine favor bestowed upon him by Aphrodite would ensure no consequences for his kidnap of Helen. He sailed into the night like a man with the backing of all the gods, but Paris would soon learn that the favor of one deity did not mean the favour of all.

Francesco Primaticcio's painting "The Abduction of Helen"

Heading to War

When Menelaus returned to Sparta and discovered Helen was gone, he flew into a rage. His servants notified him that the young prince from Troy had been the fiend who carried her off, and he immediately called upon his wise friend Odysseus to travel with him to Troy to petition her return. However, when they arrived at Troy, the Trojans informed them that there had been many precedents for not returning captives, such as the kidnapping of Medea by another Achaean.[3] Therefore, the Trojans would not release her.

---

[3] Hdt. 1.3.2

After being denied, the pair returned to Greece and set about invoking the sacred oath Helen's suitors had sworn before King Tyndareus. "He came to Agamemnon at Mycenae, and begged him to muster an army against Troy and to raise levies in Greece. And he, sending a herald to each of the kings, reminded them of the oaths which they had sworn, and warned them to look to the safety each of his own wife, saying that the affront had been offered equally to the whole of Greece."[4]

The greatest Achaean warriors came together from the distant cities of Greece in honor of the oath they had sworn. Agamemnon praised them all and Menelaus gave his thanks before the brothers gave the order to each commander in his ship to set sail for Troy.

En route to the great citadel, however, the entire fleet was plagued by storms. Ships crashed against rocks, and they almost lost their way in the squalls before finding a safe port. Calchas, the renowned seer, revealed to the commanders that they were afflicted by storms brought upon them by Artemis because Agamemnon had killed a deer sacred to her. The Achaeans asked what they should do to appease the goddess, and Calchas told them that Agamemnon must sacrifice his daughter, Iphigenia.

By this time, Agamemnon saw the war with Troy as his opportunity to immortalize his name amongst the great Achaean heroes. War-crazed and battle-starved, King Agamemnon fought off his paternal misgivings and called upon his daughter. Artemis took pity on the innocent girl, tied up like an animal for sacrifice, and — seeing the murderousness of the rapidly escalating war — swooped down and replaced Iphigenia with a lamb. "After a sacrifice to Apollo, a serpent darted from the altar beside the neighbouring plane-tree, in which there was a nest; and having consumed the eight sparrows in the nest, together with the mother bird, which made the ninth, it was turned to stone. Calchas said that this sign was given them by the will of Zeus, and he inferred from what had happened that Troy was destined to be taken in a period of ten years."[5]

Despite the prophecy from Zeus, the Achaean commanders were compelled to uphold the oath they swore to King Tyndareus, so they continued to Troy. As they neared the Trojan country, Menelaus called for the fleet to stop at the nearby island of Tenedos in the hope of reasoning, once again, with the Trojan king Priam. The embassy and the response were the same as before, but this time, the council of Trojans threatened to kill both Menelaus and Odysseus if they returned.

While the embassy was in Troy, the army grew restless. Achilles, the boy born to Thetis and Peleus after that fateful wedding in Aegina, was now 15 and already proving himself to be more skilled than most of the Achaean soldiers twice his age, including his friend Patroclus.

---

[4] Apollodorus *Epitome* E 3.6
[5] Apollodorus *Epitome* E 3.15

Achilles's presence among Agamemnon's great army was no error — it was his destiny. Zeus was not the only immortal to understand that he was condemning Thetis to an unjust marriage. Eternally youthful, Thetis had no interest in the ageing Peleus, but she followed the orders of Zeus and soon bore a child. As a demigod, the child Achilles was mortal and, furthermore, Thetis saw in his future a forked path. Either he would live a long, uneventful life and die of old age, or he would choose to take up arms and become the greatest warrior who ever lived, immortalizing his name in song and poem forever. Fearful of this fate, Thetis sneaked down to the deathly River Styx and, holding her baby by the heel, she dipped his body into the waters, thus making the remainder of his young body impervious to harm.

Peter Paul Rubens' painting "Thetis Dipping the Infant Achilles into the River Styx"

Like most heroes, however, the young Achilles was cursed with prophesies looming over his name. Calchas, before the fleet set out for Troy, implored Agamemnon to travel to Aegina in order to recruit the boy, without whom the endeavor was destined to fail. It was on the island of Tenedos, however, that Achilles sealed his fate. "They say that Achilles was strictly charged by Thetis his mother not to slay Tenes, as one that was much respected by Apollo, and that the Goddess committed the trust to one of the household servants that he should take special care and put him in mind of it, lest Achilles should kill Tenes at unawares. But when Achilles made an incursion into Tenedos and pursued the sister of Tenes, being very fair, Tenes met him and defended his sister; whereupon she escaped, but Tenes was slain. Achilles, knowing him as he fell down dead, slew his own servant, because he being present did not admonish him to the contrary."[6]

When the Achaeans could see the formidable citadel, Calchas received another premonition that the first Greek to set foot in Troy would also be the first to die. Odysseus, eager to show his valor and desirous of making the Trojans pay for Paris's actions, leapt from his ship as it arrived on the beach and bore his sword to the oncoming defenders. The Achaeans were inspired by Odysseus's selflessness and soon followed him in droves. Protesilaus was the next to land on the beach, but — after killing a handful of Trojans — he met his fate at the hands of Prince Hector. The Achaean army soon learned that Odysseus avoided the fate prophesied by Calchas by throwing down his shield before him onto the sand.

A bitter fight ensued in which the Trojans relinquished the beach to the invaders, after which the Greeks built a defensive wall and took stock of their provisions. If the gods had decreed their occupation of the Trojan beach was to last ten bloody years, the wait was unavoidable.

Nine years passed, and the Achaeans, incapable of besieging the city, took to manning their defenses, cultivating where they could, and raiding their enemy's allies as often as possible. In larceny, two Achaeans surpassed the rest. Ajax the Great was especially skilled at pillaging and Achilles, it is said, plundered no fewer than 11 cities and 12 islands allied to the Trojan cause.

---

[6] Plutarch *Moralia* 28

An ancient depiction of Ajax

Marie Lan-Nguyen's picture of a 5th century BCE depiction of Achilles and Ajax playing dice

From these cities, two women of exceptional beauty found themselves among the loot. Achilles took the lovely Briseis and Agamemnon received Chryseis, daughter of Apollo's priest Chryses, as their shares.

"Upon the priest Chryses the son of Atreus [Agamemnon] had wrought dishonour. For he had come to the swift ships of the Achaeans to free his daughter, bearing ransom past counting; and in his hands he held the wreaths of Apollo who strikes from afar, on a staff of gold; and he implored all the Achaeans, but most of all the two sons of Atreus, the marshallers of the people: 'Sons of Atreus, and other well-greaved Achaeans, to you may the gods who have homes upon Olympus grant that you sack the city of Priam, and return safe to your homes; but my dear child release to me, and accept the ransom out of reverence for the son of Zeus, Apollo who strikes from afar.'

"Then all the rest of the Achaeans shouted assent, to reverence the priest and accept the glorious ransom, yet the thing did not please the heart of Agamemnon, son of Atreus, but he sent him away harshly."[7]

A depiction of Chryses appealing to Agamemnon for his daughter

So spoke the commander of the Greek army, and the Achaeans and Trojans alike heard his impiety. Chryses, dismayed, called upon Apollo to avenge his sacrilegious treatment at the hands of Agamemnon, and the god heard his call. Arrows crowded the skies above the Achaean camp, but they were not made by Trojan hands; the angry god started with the animals, the mules and the hunting dogs, then let loose his divine arrows on the men, bringing plague to all. Before long, Agamemnon had no choice but to return Chryseis to her father.

The Achaean leader had learned not to anger Apollo, but he was not prepared to return to his position empty-handed. The soldiers received their share and Agamemnon's was greatest of all — greater even than that of the now-matured Achilles, whose prize the son of Atreus coveted. This was not a contest of skill, however, and Agamemnon had no need to prove himself against

---

[7] *Iliad* II.1.15-25

Achilles. He was the commander of the Achaean forces — any prize was his by right, and he took what he saw as his. Achilles was so enraged as he watched Odysseus walk away with Briseis that he declared neither he nor the Myrmidons under his command would fight for such a disgraceful leader. He then called on his mother Thetis to go to Zeus and implore him to bring tragedy upon the Greeks — to make them see the error of their leader's actions and to beg for the return of their greatest warrior. Thetis heard her son's plight and went to Mount Olympus to speak with the Lord of Gods.

Zeus, knowing that they were now in the portentous 10th year of his plan, sent a dream to Agamemnon. In the dream, Zeus told him that the gods of Olympus were no longer divided in their support for the combatants; they now all supported the Achaeans, and Agamemnon should again muster his forces and attack the citadel at all speed. Before doing so, however, the arrogant commander decided to test the morale of his forces. He needed to know that they trusted him as much as the gods, so he told them to leave the land of Troy for their homes. He told them that their campaign was over and they could return to their wives and children, which the Greek forces accepted with delight. They began loading the ships and preparing their departure until Hera, furious at her husband's actions, appealed to Athena. The two victims of Paris's judgment were still furious at the snub, and Athena answered Hera's call and came down from lofty Olympus to speak to Odysseus, who was standing dejected on the beach. "Son of Laërtes, sprung from Zeus, Odysseus of many wiles, is it thus indeed that ye will fling yourselves on your benched ships to flee to your dear native land? Aye, and ye would leave to Priam and the Trojans their boast, even Argive Helen, for whose sake many an Achaean hath perished in Troy, far from his dear native land. But go thou now throughout the host of the Achaeans, and hold thee back no more; and with thy gentle words seek thou to restrain every man, neither suffer them to draw into the sea their curved ships."[8]

Odysseus sprang to action, running along the shore and admonishing his countrymen as they packed up their wares. He called out their cowardice and lack of pride, and he reminded the kings and princes of the oaths they had sworn before the gods that fateful day in Sparta. Most of the Greeks were swayed by his reasoning, and soon they were mustered for battle again.

The princes in Troy deployed their forces, but as they were leaving the citadel, Hector turned to his brother — the bringer of 10 years of sorrow to his countrymen — and admonished him for not doing everything in his power to deliver his people from further bloodshed. Paris understood and was shamed into placing himself before the front line of the Trojan forces and calling to Menelaus. He challenged Menelaus to end the war in one-on-one combat. The cuckolded king agreed, and the two drew their arms.

---

[8] *Iliad 2.169-181*

"Hector Admonishes Paris for His Softness and Exhorts Him to Go to War", by J.H.W. Tischbein

The two armies watched as the king and prince approached, and from the start it was an unevenly matched fight; Menelaus, the better warrior, sent Paris crashing to the ground again and again. The wily Aphrodite watched from Mount Olympus as her champion was pummeled to the ground over and over. She saw the fate of Paris if he continued to place himself before Menelaus's sword, so she swooped down to the battlefield and whisked him away before Menelaus could deliver the fatal blow.

The forces stood watching, dumbstruck at the supernatural events taking place before their eyes, but while the mortals were paralyzed into inaction, the immortals raged at Aphrodite's brazenness. Hera flew to her husband; in her fury, she demanded he make amends for the goddess's actions. Zeus heeded his wife's grievances and intervened. Pandarus, a Trojan archer in the front line, stood with an arrow trapped between his trembling fingers, awaiting a commander to tell him the duel-truce had been lifted. However, thanks to Zeus, his grip loosened and a single arrow escaped the Trojan ranks. The arrow broke the skin of Menelaus's leg and the truce between the forces. After that, the two armies charged.

Zeus's heroes fulfilled his desire, and in the melee, they reached their full, bloodthirsty potential. Diomedes brought murderous slaughter upon the Trojan ranks. They fell in droves at his sword, including the unfortunate Pandarus, until he reached Aeneas, son of the crippled prince Anchises. Anchises had once been a handsome and heroic prince, so much so in fact that Aphrodite had chosen to lay with him. When the foolish prince later boasted of his exploits, the goddess of love crippled him in retaliation, but when their son was about to fall under the sword of Diomedes, Aphrodite descended upon the battlefield again to save one of her favorites.

William Blake Richmond's painting of Aphrodite and Anchises

Diomedes was enraged. All thoughts of cosmological rank, all sentiments of pious obeisance, were torn asunder by his fury, and the hero recalled the prayer that was answered by Athena on the battlefield. "Wherefore now if any god come hither to make trial of thee, do not thou in any wise fight face to face with any other immortal gods, save only if Aphrodite, daughter of Zeus, shall enter the battle, her do thou smite with a thrust of the sharp bronze."[9]

In his rage he now felt justified, morally and divinely, in taking his great spear and swinging it at the goddess. He pierced her divine skin just above her palm, and she cried out and dropped her son. Apollo saw the effrontery and stepped in to protect Aeneas from Diomedes's wrath. Iris flew to the battlefield and rescued Aphrodite, who was still bleeding the heavenly ichor that runs through the gods' veins. Diomedes called out to her as she fled: "Keep thee away, daughter of Zeus, from war and fighting. Sufficeth it not that thou beguilest weakling women? But if into battle thou wilt enter, verily methinks thou shalt shudder at the name thereof, if thou hearest it even from afar."[10]

[9] *Iliad 5.131*
[10] *Iliad 5.351*

On her way to Olympus, Aphrodite came across Ares leaning against his spear on a cloud and watching the bloody proceedings below. She implored him to lend her his chariot to reach their home more quickly, and he agreed without argument. Once she arrived in Olympus, she decried the Achaeans, telling the other gods and goddesses that their transgressions knew no bounds now that they were prepared to attack even the gods. Athena simply laughed at the beautiful goddess and turned to her father and mocked her. Zeus told Aphrodite that her place was in the marital bedchamber, not the battlefield, and recommended she take no further part in the war. The other gods would not heed the advice; emboldened by the heat of the battle, they traded artifice for expediency in their machinations.

Meanwhile, Diomedes's wrath had not abated, and when he saw Aeneas being protected in plain sight by Apollo, he leapt upon him three times, even as his efforts were shaken off by the god each time. On the fourth attack, Apollo turned to him. With a mighty scream, he reminded Diomedes that he was not immortal and shared nothing of their glory or worthiness. Diomedes's wrath subsided briefly, and he gave way to the god as Apollo whisked Aeneas away to his temple on Pergamus. There, Leto and Artemis awaited the hero and healed him in the sanctuary.

As the battled raged below, Apollo flew to the cloud on which stood the bane of humanity and admonished Ares for allowing Diomedes such liberties in the face of the gods. Ares still stood, leaning on his spear with the nonchalance only the god of war could show in the face of such a bloody battle, and Apollo said to him, "Ares, Ares, thou bane of mortals, thou blood-stained stormer of walls, wilt thou not now enter into the battle and withdraw this man therefrom, this son of Tydeus, who now would fight even against father Zeus?"[11]

Ares agreed with Apollo that Diomedes had gone far enough and needed to be controlled. Apollo flew down to join his mother and sister in his temple on Pergamus, while Ares landed amidst the Trojan ranks disguised as the leader of the Thracian allies. In the voice of Acamas, he set about admonishing the Trojans for their inability to keep one Achaean constrained. His divine words roused the spirits of the other men and they turned to their leader, Prince Hector.

The Achaeans also mustered their courage, and Diomedes turned to his allies with Odysseus at his side and inspired in them renewed spirit for war. Fighting resumed, and it was unmatched for its brutality. Aeneas rejoined his comrades after Apollo saw that Athena had left the battlefield. He was not sure where the goddess had gone, but he felt sure that Aeneas was now safe from her meddling, and he knew the Trojans desperately needed him.

With Ares at his side, Hector fell upon the Achaeans, killing them in droves, but it was Diomedes who saw through the Thracian guise. He turned to his men and told them to give ground; like the cowardly Paris and Aeneas, Hector too had a god at his side — and none other

---

[11] *Iliad* 5.458-459

than the god of war — to help them gain unfair advantage. The Achaeans took Diomedes at his word and gave ground, carefully facing their enemy with his dreaded aid.

On Olympus, Hera turned to Athena, bringing her attention to Ares's unfair actions and admonishing her as the goddess of war: "Out upon it, thou child of Zeus that beareth the aegis, unwearied one, verily it was for naught that we pledged our word to Menelaus, that not until he had sacked well-walled Ilios should he get him home, if we are to suffer baneful Ares thus to rage. Nay, come, let us twain likewise bethink us of furious valour."[12]

Athena heard the queen of the gods and she agreed; Ares had gone too far and had to be stopped. She went to the hall of Zeus and found her gleaming armor with the ferocious Aegis that would strike fear into any foe that saw it. While there, she turned to Zeus and asked if he agreed with Ares's actions, seeing as how he had professed to be neutral throughout the proceedings and had refused to judge the fairest of the goddesses himself. "Then in answer spake to her Zeus, the cloud-gatherer: 'Nay, come now, rouse against him Athena, driver of the spoil, who has ever been wont above others to bring sore pain upon him.'"[13]

Athena left Zeus sitting atop his throne, majestic and seemingly disinterested. Hera had mounted her chariot and was awaiting her; the two flew down to the battlefield and, now in the guise of the warrior Stentor, Hera called out to the Achaeans by her side. "Fie, ye Argives, base things of shame fair in semblance only! So long as goodly Achilles was wont to fare into battle, never would the Trojans come forth even before the Dardanian gate; for of his mighty spear had they dread; but now far from the city they are fighting at the hollow ships."[14]

The Achaeans had been driven back so far away from the city that they were fighting near their ships, moored on the shore where they had spent the past 10 years. Now however, they were inspired by the goddess's words and began to fight back. Athena turned to Diomedes, who was wiping the blood from a small wound he'd received from Pandarus, and scolded him. Athena told him that he had forgotten the face of his father Tydeus, and that he was probably not even a son of that great warrior if he was willing to slink away from the battlefield so easily. Diomedes recognised her as the immortal she was and told her there was no point joining the fight if Ares was on the battlefield. Athena admonished him for being so afraid and told him that Ares had implied to her and Hera that he would come down to the battlefield in aid of the Achaeans. As it turned out, however, Ares had turned on the Greeks in favor of supporting those that his lover, Aphrodite, supported.

Diomedes now stood on his swift chariot and the axels groaned as Athena boarded beside him. They drove at Ares, and when the god realized Diomedes was almost upon him, he sent a spear flying towards the great soldier. Athena caught the spear with one hand, however, and helped

---

[12] *Iliad* 5. 712-718
[13] *Iliad* 5.764
[14] *Iliad* 5.791

Diomedes return the blow once they were close enough. Diomedes's own spear tore at the flesh of Ares's stomach, and the god screamed louder than the two armies combined. Pain swirled with shocked insult in the god's voice, and he disappeared from the battlefield immediately to emerge bleeding at the side of his father Zeus.

After that, the fighting continued without the gods. Just before night fell, Prince Hector and Ajax the Great met each other in battle. A duel ensued in which neither one gained the upper hand over the other; fairly matched, they continued until the light was too dim for anybody to bear swords on another, and both armies retired for the night.

The Achaeans consolidated their forces, burned what dead they could bring back with them to the ships, and waited for morning. Meanwhile, the Trojans argued bitterly amongst themselves. With Paris in their midst, they demanded he give back the wife of Menelaus, but the young prince would not agree. He offered the treasure which he took from Sparta when he kidnapped its queen and more still, but he would not part with Helen herself; she had been given to him by Aphrodite and it seemed no amount of his kin's blood could soften his heart when it came to her.

The next day, both armies called a truce in order to clear the battlefield of their dead and to bury them honorably. On Olympus, Zeus had seen enough of the gods fighting and now forbade them from doing so any longer. Henceforth, he would see how the mortal heroes rose to the challenges at Troy.

When the fighting resumed, the Greeks did not fare well. The Trojans fought them back to the makeshift wall they built to defend their ships, and following these losses, Agamemnon swallowed his pride and gave in to Achilles. He sent Briseis to his tent with the purpose of inspiring him back to the battle, but Achilles remained unmoved.

Despite the success of clandestine night attacks on the sleeping Trojans and their allies by Diomedes and Odysseus, the next morning brought more tragedy to the Achaeans in the bitter fighting. By the end of the day, it seemed nobody was spared of injury in the Achaean camp, including Diomedes, Odysseus, and even the great commander Agamemnon. Achilles, curious about the effects of his mother's words to Zeus, asked his companion Patroclus to go to Agamemnon's tent. While he was there, the whole host of injured and pained Greeks compelled him to convince Achilles to come to their aid, and Patroclus pitied them all.

In the coming days, Achilles was still unmoved despite the Trojans advancing beyond the Greek defensive wall and battling around their ships. Hera, growing increasingly exasperated by her husband's prohibition, decided to take measures to ensure the Trojans did not win the war. "Then she took thought, the ox-eyed, queenly Hera, how she might beguile the mind of Zeus that beareth the aegis. And this plan seemed to her mind the best—to go to Ida, when she had beauteously adorned her person, if so be he might desire to lie by her side and embrace her body in love, and she might shed a warm and gentle sleep upon her eyelids and his cunning mind."[15]

She called upon Aphrodite and asked that the goddess of love give her love and desire to take with her to her husband's bed. Aphrodite found no reason to withhold her skills from her queen, and she agreed. That night, Hera succeeded in her attempts and Zeus fell into a sleep so deep that Poseidon seized the opportunity to lend his support to the ailing Greeks.

When Zeus awoke, he realized that he had been duped and not only gave permission to Apollo to help the Trojans, but sent him down to the battlefield himself. With Apollo's help, the Trojans breached the Achaeans' defensive wall and reached the Greek ships. At this point, Patroclus could no longer bear to witness the destruction in silence. He turned to Achilles and begged him to join the battle and, if he would not, to at least allow him to lead the Myrmidons against the Trojans, who had now begun to burn the Greek ships. Achilles finally relented to his companion and lent him his own armor to bring fear to the Trojans.

The effect of Achilles's armor on the battlefield was decisive. Patroclus killed many of the best Trojan warriors and, believing they were seeing their greatest warrior return to the field, the rest of the Achaeans took up the fight with extra vigor. The Trojans fell back to their mighty walls, as Patroclus led the Greeks forward. "Then would the sons of the Achaeans have taken high-gated Troy by the hands of Patroclus, for around and before him he raged with his spear, had not Phoebus Apollo taken his stand upon the well-builded wall thinking thoughts of bane for him, but bearing aid to the Trojans. Thrice did Patroclus set foot upon a corner of the high wall, and thrice did Apollo fling him back, thrusting against the bright shield with his immortal hands. But when for the fourth time he rushed on like a god, then with a terrible cry Apollo spake to him winged words: 'Give back, Zeus-born Patroclus. It is not fated, I tell thee, that by thy spear the city of the lordly Trojans shall be laid waste, nay, nor by that of Achilles, who is better far than thou.'"

The battle around Patroclus grew fierce and every great hero was hit with blows from all sides. Once he had taken a step back from the god, Patroclus fell into a duel with Hector, and the two of them were so evenly matched that they ended up falling away from each other and joining the throngs of soldiers around them. Patroclus turned to his foes three times, each time striking dead three Trojan warriors. On the fourth leap, however, Apollo once again stepped into the maul and put an end to Patroclus's success. He struck Patroclus first in the back, knocking him down, then across the helmet, sending it rattling away from him. At this point, brave Euphorbus hurled a spear at Patroclus, wounding him; but Patroclus was not yet defeated. He started to retreat into the ranks of his comrades, but he was spotted by Hector, and with one final thrust of the spear, Patroclus lay dead in the shadow of the walls he had hoped to bring down.

---

[15] *Iliad 14.165*

An ancient relief depicting the body of Patroclus being lifted by Menelaus and Meriones
while Odysseus and others look on

Nikolai Ge's painting, "Achilles Lamenting the Death of Patroclus"

Achilles was understandably distraught. Patroclus's body was brought back in the Achaeans' camp, and the entire army mourned the loss of such a great soldier. Though they burned his body and ate a feast in his honour, Achilles fasted. His mother Thetis, knowing that Achilles was fated to die if he killed Hector, tried once more to protect her son from his fate. She appealed to the great god Hephaestus to make Achilles the greatest armor he had ever made, in the hope that it would protect him.

A picture of Thetis giving Achilles armor forged by Hephaestus

With this armor on his back, Achilles joined the battle, but as he watched Achilles tear through the Trojan ranks with ferocity, Zeus knew that he had to bring a balance to the war. There was no glory in a massacre, so he called upon the goddess Themis and told her to gather all of the gods and bring them to his palace. When all had arrived, Zeus told them he was lifting his previous prohibition on fighting and encouraged them to take whichever side they preferred to restore glory and honor to the battle. "So spake the son of Cronos, and roused war unabating. And the gods went their way into the battle, being divided in counsel: Hera gat her to the gathering of the ships, and with her Pallas Athena, and Poseidon, the Shaker of Earth, and the helper Hermes, that was beyond all in the cunning of his mind; and together with these went Hephaestus, exulting in his might, halting, but beneath him his slender legs moved nimbly; but unto the Trojans went Ares, of the flashing helm, and with him Phoebus [Apollo], of the unshorn locks, and Artemis, the archer, and Leto and Xanthus and laughter-loving Aphrodite."[16]

---

[16] *Iliad* 20.30-40

Those who took the side of the Achaeans cleared the way for Achilles to smite the Trojans in his search for Patroclus's killer. Achilles killed and threw the corpses of so many of the Trojans into the River Scamander that the god of the river himself rose up to fight him, but still Achilles gave no ground. When it seemed Achilles might fall to the river god, Hephaestus attacked the god with a firestorm so great that Hera had to call him off quickly, lest it spread through all the rivers of the land.

The battle soon turned from men to gods, each turning their hands onto the other — brother against sister, mother against son. Ares, his position as god of war bringing him confidence, took to the goddess of wisdom, Athena, with bloody arms. The fight was bitter between the two until Ares vanquished her defenses and landed the sharp tip of his spear on the Aegis at her chest. However, this Aegis could protect her from the lightning of Zeus himself, and Athena retaliated with a blow that sent the god flying into the dust. "'Fool,' said Athena, 'not even yet hast thou learned how much mightier than thou I avow me to be, that thou matchest thy strength with mine. On this wise shalt thou satisfy to the full the Avengers invoked of thy mother, who in her wrath deviseth evil against thee, for that thou hast deserted the Achaeans and bearest aid to the overweening Trojans.'"[17]

This was the end for the Trojan contingent of gods. One by one, they were chastised by Hera, reminded of their positions on Olympus, and told to give up their hubris and come back to the fold. Hera reminded them all of the divine order, and they left the battlefield to the mortals — all except Apollo. The god feared for his Trojans still, and as they retreated to the safety of their walls, he disguised himself and led Achilles away from the open doors into the open plane. When he finally revealed himself to the hero, the doors were closed and all except Hector, too ashamed to retreat, were safe behind the gates. This would be the last mistake Hector would make.

---

[17] *Iliad* 21.414

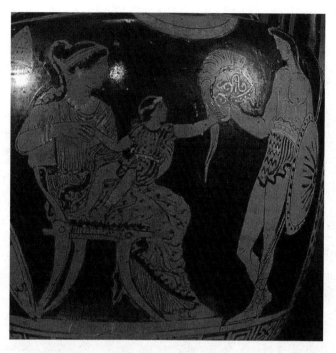

An ancient depiction of Hector's last visit with his wife, Andromache, and infant son Astyanax, who is startled by his father's helmet

Zeus considers saving Hector a third time, but Athena convinces her father that Hector's fate has been decided. After a brief battle, Achilles killed Hector. Before his death, Hector pleads with Achilles to return his body for a proper burial, but Achilles refuses and mocks him by dragging his body through the dirt and letting his men repeatedly stab Hector's corpse. This show just how consumed Achilles is by rage. Priam and Hecuba witness this from within the city walls, distraught over their son's death.

"Achilles Slays Hector", by Peter Paul Rubens

Achilles continues abusing Hector's body, but Apollo intervenes by protecting the body from further harm or decay. Apollo eventually convinced Zeus that Achilles must give Hector's body back. Zeus agrees and gets Thetis to convince Achilles that this is what he must do, while at the same time sending Iris to inform Priam that he is to go and get his son's body. The gods allow Priam safe passage to the camp and he pleads with Achilles. Priam finally convinces Achilles to return the body by drawing on the warrior's connection with his own father.

After the gods took their leave of the battlefield, the course of the war continued much in the same way. Allies arrived for the Trojans in increasing strength, including the contingent of Amazons whose queen, Penthesilea, Achilles slew and fell in love with as he removed her bloody helmet. The gods, once divided by either pride or interest, were united again once they saw the destruction Achilles continued to wreak; he had avenged Patroclus's death, but his anger was still not sated. Thus, in an attack on the city in which Achilles broke through the defenses, Apollo was given permission to guide an arrow from Paris's bow to strike Achilles in the place where Thetis held him as a baby in the River Styx. Achilles was killed, but not by a mortal's hand, thus leaving his honor intact.

Since the *Iliad* tells almost the entire story of the end of the Trojan War, many readers who are either unfamiliar with Homer's epics or have not read them in awhile often mistakenly think that the *Iliad* ends with the Greeks' use of the Trojan Horse to capture and burn Troy. In fact, the climactic final battle, Achilles' death, and the destruction of Troy all occur at the beginning of the Odyssey.

In the final days of Troy, the Achaeans received three more prophecies that would determine their success. "To wit, first, if the bones of Pelops were brought to them; next, if Neoptolemus fought for them; and third, if the Palladium, which had fallen from heaven, were stolen from Troy, for while it was within the walls the city could not be taken."[18]

Odysseus once again took the lead and ensured that each of the objects was retrieved, even sneaking into Troy disguised as a beggar to steal the Palladium. Although he was not the chief commander of the Achaeans, Odysseus guaranteed their success at Troy by devising the famous Trojan Horse, lamented by Aeneas after he escaped his burning city.

"Ourselves did make

a breach within our walls and opened wide

the ramparts of our city. One and all

were girded for the task. Smooth-gliding wheels

were 'neath its feet; great ropes stretched round its neck,

till o'er our walls the fatal engine climbed,

pregnant with men-at-arms. On every side

fair youths and maidens made a festal song,

and hauled the ropes with merry heart and gay.

So on and up it rolled, a tower of doom,

and in proud menace through our Forum moved.

... Cassandra then

---

[18] Apollodorus *Epitome* E 5.10

from heaven-instructed heart our doom foretold;

but doomed to unbelief were Ilium's sons.

Our hapless nation on its dying day

flung free o'er streets and shrines the votive flowers."[19]

"The Procession of the Trojan Horse in Troy", by Giovanni Domenico Tiepolo

---

[19] *Aenead* 2.234-250

A 7th century BCE depiction of the Trojan Horse, the oldest known depiction yet found

The Trojans ignored the fate of Laocoön and his sons, who had been eaten by a mighty serpent from the sea after they warned against bringing the ill-fated horse in to the city. After they had celebrated their victory and were quietly sleeping off their libations, the Greek fleet returned from its cunning hiding place on the nearby island of Tenedos, stepped through the breach in the city walls, and slaughtered their unwitting foes. Spoils were divided between the commanders, and the great city of Troy was razed to the ground.

Once the Achaeans had taken what they believed to be theirs by divine right, and vengeance had been taken on the memory of Hector by throwing his infant son Astyanax from the city walls, they left. Each leader headed back his own kingdom, and for the most part, their fates were their own. The actions of Agamemnon, Odysseus, and Diomedes throughout the Trojan War afforded them fame and glory, and the gods took no more vengeance upon them for what happened there.

What came after the war — hubris enacted, insults hurled — was another matter, and this demarcation of "war" and "return" was a luxury the gods did not afford Ajax the Lesser, however. During the looting of the city, Ajax the Lesser not only claimed the prophetess

Cassandra as part of his spoils, he also raped her on Athena's altar. For this reason, Athena ensured he never returned home, smashing his ship on the rocks and sealing his ignominious, if merited, fate.

Logistics

It may help readers to take a brief look at the logistics of war during this period when trying to understand the overall narrative. One of the main issues is the 'Ten Year Gap" between the Greeks landing on the beach at Troy and finally burning it to the ground. Since very little appears to have happened during this period, and the answer of "prophecy" pushed the limits of the fantastic, this question was one debated by the ancient Greeks as well. After Herodotus wrote his *Histories*, almost as full of fanciful action as the *Iliad*, Thucydides wrote the much more sober *History of the Peloponnesian War*. Famous for including nearly no mention of gods nor prophecies, Thucydides's interests lay in the political machinations and the very real logistics of warfare. He came to a logical conclusion as to why the city of Troy was not captured much earlier: "And this was due not so much to scarcity of men as of money. Difficulty of subsistence made the invaders reduce the numbers of the army to a point at which it might live on the country during the prosecution of the war. Even after the victory they obtained on their arrival—and a victory there must have been, or the fortifications of the naval camp could never have been built— there is no indication of their whole force having been employed; on the contrary, they seem to have turned to cultivation of the Chersonese and to piracy from want of supplies. This was what really enabled the Trojans to keep the field for ten years against them; the dispersion of the enemy making them always a match for the detachment left behind. If they had brought plenty of supplies with them, and had persevered in the war without scattering for piracy and agriculture, they would have easily defeated the Trojans in the field; since they could hold their own against them with the division on service. In short, if they had stuck to the siege, the capture of Troy would have cost them less time and less trouble. But as want of money proved the weakness of earlier expeditions, so from the same cause even the one in question, more famous than its predecessors, may be pronounced on the evidence of what it effected to have been inferior to its renown and to the current opinion about it formed under the tuition of the poets."[20]

The style of warfare employed in the *Iliad* is often a source of confusion for readers as well, mostly because it should not be confused with that employed by the Spartans at Thermopylae or the Athenians at Marathon. Hoplite warfare, the style of warfare used by the Greeks during the Persian Wars in the Classical era, is typified by the phalanx formation, in which the soldiers fought with spears behind interlocked shields (known as "hoplons," after which the style of warfare is named).

The method employed in the Trojan War is very different, however, and suited the needs of the narrative more than any military tactical advantage. The warriors in the Trojan War also

---

[20] Thuc. *The Peloponnesian War* 1.11

generally fought one-on-one, especially if they were the great heroes. Again, this is a narrative technique; lauding the coordination of a phalanx is not nearly as appealing as the duels that take place several times in the *Iliad*. The duel between Paris and Menelaus, for example, allowed the narrator to extol the fighting abilities of each soldier and introduce the divine intervention that would force both armies to engage again after 10 years.

In the narrative, there are instances of chariot warfare (when Diomedes attacks Ares, for instance), which was also a common theme in pre-hoplite warfare. If the ability to buy armor was a source of pride and social status — and given the episodes in the *Iliad* in which the surrounding soldiers fought over the armor of a fallen comrade, this is clearly true — then the ability to buy a chariot would have been an instant symbol of greatness for whoever was riding in one. Thatwould have been apparent to the ancient reader.

Myth, Legend, or Folktale?

Determining the historicity of the Trojan War and the account in the *Iliad* is obviously crucial. Is the modern reader supposed to accept that the ancient reader or listener believed Apollo hit Patroclus in the back, causing him to fall and be killed? Should the modern reader accept that even the ancients took their myths with a grain of salt? These questions are like the bodies of hydras — each springing more questions as answers are attempted until they eventually reach such enormity as "What is religion?".

Today, there is very little doubt that some battle did take place on a site in Turkey that was most probably Troy. Throughout the vast expanse of centuries that separate the event from today, there have been numerous references connecting Troy to this area, and there is no shortage of "historicizing" in the Iliad itself.[21] But debating the location or existence of such a battle takes a backseat when looking at the legends contained within the *Iliad*; in the epic poem, the narrative about the Trojan War is considered to be almost unequivocally a legend.

Scholars of Grimm's fairy tales, however, know all too well the difficulty in isolating some stories as "legends" and others as "folktales." Great stories develop the qualities of flypaper throughout their lives; they develop, over time and cultural space, and they metamorphose. They are changed slightly with every new telling in the oral tradition. For example, the emergence of the "wicked stepmother" in Grimm's collected fairy tales came about after the initial publication of their tales garnered a swathe of letters from concerned mothers who had noticed that most of the "evil" characters were mothers, resulting in the move to make them stepmothers instead.[22]

From a cursory reading of the *Iliad* and the later sources for the war, it is easy to see how it may have been amended for entertainment purposes, resulting in its legendary qualities. The role of the gods in the story of the Trojan War is most interesting, as it represents the culmination of

---

[21] Kirk 1996
[22] Tatar & Byatt 2012

their formation as entities. Their role is primarily that of "stimuli" for heroic action.[23] The story begins with Zeus wanting to instigate heroic deeds, seemingly for his own entertainment. Instead of simply accepting her success in winning Paris's judgment, Aphrodite ignites the fire of war by offering Paris the woman of the man who forgot to honor her. Before long, gods and goddesses are swooping down to save their favorites and, in the case of Paris's duel with Menelaus, prolonging the already drawn out war. The gods are used by Zeus to instigate, balance, and eventually end the war he wanted to see; but ultimately, they just add magnificence to what is essentially a legendary narrative of a perceived past event.[24]

It is also easy to forget when these colorful legendary or mythological characters "lived," and not surprisingly, given the nature of myth and its involvement in historical, cultural, and religious walks of life, there is confusion around an exact chronology. That said, Hesiod's Ages of Man can help to gain a broad perspective. According to Hesiod's poem *Works and Days*, written around the 7th century BCE (the same time as Homer's writings), humans have been through five "stages" of existence:

1. The Golden Age. This took place during Chronos's rule before that of Zeus. In this time, mankind knew neither strife nor toil and they lived to an exceptionally old age, dying in peace and remaining on earth as spirits (daemons).

2. The Silver Age. This age of mankind did not live as long as the previous generation, but their childhoods were over 100 years. It took place during the change of rule between Chronos and his son Zeus, but mankind was impious and Zeus destroyed them because they would not worship the gods.

3. The Bronze Age. This age was when mankind was at its hardiest and most bellicose. Still impious and with a mind only for war on each other, Zeus destroyed this generation with the great flood. Only Deucalion and his wife Pyrrha survived.

4. The Heroic Age. Most of the heroes known to Greek myth lived during this age — after the flood and before the "common" age of mankind. The heroes still coexisted with the gods and both took part in the great wars at Thebes and Troy.

5. The Iron Age. This was the age in which Hesiod believed he lived. He describes it in typical fashion against the backdrop of ages free from toil, full of fantasy, heroic deeds, and the constant (and often tangible) presence of the gods. It is, essentially, the "debased" age, full of woe, turmoil, and broken expectations.

The story of the Trojan War is essentially the story of men fighting on the impulse of the gods, so the history of those men in Hesiod's context should be emphasized. It is worth emphasizing

---

[23] Kirk 1996
[24] ibid.

the chronology of the Heroic Age in this case, as the stories within generally revolve around the great "tribal" families of the Mycenaean Palace Period, centering on places such as Argos, Mycenae, Thebes, Athens, Aegina, Claydon, Iolcus, Corinth, Sparta and Crete.[25] These cultural centres spawned the emergent stories of Greek myth, from the flood Deucalion survived to Agamemnon's war at Troy. Stories such as that of Danaus led to the story of Bellerophon and the birth of Perseus to Danae and Zeus later on. Also, the stories of the Perseid dynasty, which began with Pelops, son of the ill-fated Tantalus, led to the stories of Atreus and his sons Agamemnon and Menelaus. It is also worth bearing in mind that the stories at Troy were not the first concerning the sacking of the city by the Greeks; Hercules had sacked it a generation earlier. This vague chronology clarifies the placement of both the "historical" moment of the war in the minds of the ancient Greeks, as well as a kind of thematic formation of the gods in ancient Greek religion.

In fact, by the Trojan War, particularly the events depicted in the *Iliad*, the gods are presented "with as little fantasy as possible," as historian G.S. Kirk noted. "They are supermen and superwomen with special powers of instant travel and remote operation - they are an extra dimension of action and dramatic source of motivation."

Themes

Kirk studied the Greek myths in comparison with those in surrounding cultures and came to several interesting conclusions that shed light on the role of the gods in the story of the Trojan War. Tracing their ancestry back to the dawn of the cosmos, he wrote that the natural emergence and separation of the gods from their original "nature-gods" comprises the major part of the mythical activity of the gods. "As for the gods," he asserted, "once they have achieved their form and functions most of them are quite limited in their actions."[26]

Writing at more or less the same time, Homer and Hesiod formalized and cemented the role of the gods. There are elaborations made by later playwrights in Athens, such as Euripedes, but by the time of the Trojan War, the roles of the myths are established to such a degree that their actions mostly serve as elements of fantasy to folkloric themes.

Kirk divides the most common themes in Greek Heroic myths into 24 categories. Five he considers to be very specific to key myths (such as "Enclosure or imprisonment in a chest, jar or tomb"). Another five concern disputes within the family, such as "Deceitful Daughters," that don't really concern the story of the Trojan War. The remainder are incorporated into the Trojan War, including the most folkloric or legendary elements.

    1.   Tricks, riddles, ingenious solutions to dilemmas. Naturally, one name comes to mind when ingenuity is mentioned in the same context as myth — Odysseus. From his

---

[25] ibid.
[26] 1996

solution to Tyndareus's problem to the Trojan Horse, Odysseus is on equal par with Oedipus for ingenuity. Kirk notes that there is a certain intrinsic value in this theme, which is the reason for its presence in so many Greek myths and, indeed, many folktales worldwide.

2.   Transformations. There are some ambiguous moments in the case of gods speaking with humans, but they generally take on the shape of either an animal (a swan, in the case of Helen's birth) or a fellow warrior on either side.

3.   Accidental killing of a relative, lover, or friend. This theme is exemplified when Achilles falls in love with his female counterpart in the form of the great Amazonian warrior Penthesilea.

4.   Giants, monsters, snakes. The brutal final scene involving Laocöon's death is iconic in the story of Troy's fall. Most often, they signify some kind of natural, chthonic force; however, the Greeks tended to opt for borrowing the style of their monsters (multi-headed and/or snakelike) from those myths from the Near East that permeated their culture long before Homer's writings.

5.   Fulfilling a task or quest. This theme is the fundamental core of the Trojan War myth.

6.   Contests. The Judgement of Paris results in Paris winning Helen as much as Aphrodite winning the Apple of Discord.

7.   Punishment of impiety. This theme is displayed in all three goddesses' actions as a result of Paris's judgement, including Aphrodite's revenge on Menelaus.

8.   Killing or attempting to kill one's own child. This theme is demonstrated when Agamemnon attempts to kill his daughter Iphigenia.

9.   Revenge by murdering a man's children. According to one version of the story, the murder of Hector's son Astyanax is an example of this, rather than simply a matter of ensuring against revenge.

10.   Special weapons. Thetis's fear for her son results in her trying to equip him with the very best armour made by Hephaestus, a description of which occupies an entire book of the Iliad.[27]

---

[27] see *Book 18*

11.   Prophets and seers. This summarised version of the Trojan War would have been impossible without the countless examples of prophecy. The seer Calchas alone is responsible for much of the early decisions of the Achaeans.

12.   Mortal lovers of goddesses and gods. Anchises's affair with Aphrodite not only results in her flight to the battlefield to protect her son Aeneas, but later serves as the basis of one of Rome's foundation myths.

13.   Unusual births. Helen's presence in the story of the war goes far beyond the fact that she was inhumanly beautiful. As the daughter of Zeus, her beauty was therefore divine. This popular narrative tool is put to exceptional use here since, considering the combination of divine beauty with Aphrodite's gift, the Greeks could forgive Paris's actions to some degree.

There is another folkloristic element to the narrative of the *Iliad* — the use of repetition. In the narrative, Diomedes and Patroclus are depicted as "falling on" their foe "three times" and "rebuffed" on the fourth time. This repetition is most likely a remnant of the *Iliad*'s roots in the oral tradition.[28] Like most folktales, *the* Iliad employs this use of the number three in order to encourage memorization and create narrative tension. Patroclus fell upon his enemy and killed "three times three" Trojans before he was struck down by the god, further adding to the narrative theme of rebuffing a soldier who is too successful, as Achilles was after the death of Hector.

The story of the Trojan War, unlike some earlier myths, can be read not so much as an exercise in finding deeper meanings such as societal concerns (death and the causes of natural phenomena like earthquakes and lightning) or the birth of cult rituals, but as an exercise in examination of narrative themes and techniques. By analyzing the myth in such a thematic way, the modern reader "achieves an understanding of an inner essence by the analytical description of outward appearances."[29]

How Could the Ancient Greeks Have Worshiped These Gods?

This question is a fair one when posed by the modern reader, particularly one who has grown up in a monotheistic culture. To that reader, the gods of the ancient Greeks are fickle, capricious, mean, envious, and — for lack of a better word — human. There have been many theories tackling this confusion over the past two centuries, but one in particular seems just specific enough to be revelatory yet expansive enough to include most religious facets of the ancient Greeks. It was posed by Jean-Pierre Vernant, who stated that, to the ancient Greeks, "the gods are no more all-powerful or omniscient than they are eternal."[30] This theory is best explained in

---

[28] Propp 1968
[29] ibid.
[30] 1996

terms of a three-part theological and socio-cultural cycle including hierarchy, non-individual "powers," and society.

To the ancient Greeks, Zeus was the head of the hierarchy of natural order, and it is worth recalling how he came to occupy that position. Most modern scholars no longer equate Zeus's pantheon of gods to "natural forces," despite the fact that they are often ostensibly connected (Zeus is tied to thunder, for instance). However, they do acknowledge that Zeus's pantheon was borne of natural forces in the garb of the earliest celestial beings, such as Ouranos and Gaia.

Zeus was forced to rebel against his father Chronos and fight a battle to acquire the power the ancient Greeks allotted to him. His position as head of the family of the gods was now immovable, particularly after he negated the prophecies that beleaguered his father and grandfather with his cunning. Each god beneath him represented a key cog in the workings of the cosmic hierarchy.

However, two areas of confusion often arise from this simplification. The first is the role of fate or destiny with regard to Zeus's position at the top of the hierarchy. Readers of ancient history often find Zeus changing fate for his own ends, but at other times Zeus seems to accept that his hands are tied in that very same respect. Vernant argued that this is a misunderstanding of how the Greeks viewed fate or destiny. The ancient Greeks perceived these forces as unfixed and subject to external factors, such as the ire or desire of alternate forces. Zeus may be able to change fate in certain circumstances, but, in the case of saving his son Sarpedon in the Trojan War, his desire was outbalanced by external factors and he had to accept his son's fate.

This example gives rise to the other area of confusion — that of Zeus ceding power and decisions to the other gods who are presumably "beneath" him in the cosmic hierarchy. The important thing to remember here is that Zeus's victories, which afforded him the exalted position to which he rose, were hard-won and often depended on the help of allies. In the case of Sarpedon, Zeus wanted to save his son, but Hera told him that the other gods would not agree, as it could lead to each god saving his or her son or daughter according to their whims and not, as must be expected even for the king of the gods, to the "natural law of order." Zeus did not change the fate of his son because he saw the wisdom in having the gods on his side, despite the fact that he was stronger than each of them and commanded the throne of the heavens. Making a connection between this power structure and later feudalism has its merits.

It may help the modern reader to view the ancient Greek deities less as individuals and more like the components of a language. These gods represented not only natural phenomena but also societal aspects, their interconnectivity and multiplicity being the key to their understanding.

The ancient Greeks rarely made a distinction between singular and plural in reference to a particular god. Each god had different aspects, often described by use of an epithet. For instance, when a king was beseeched by an exile from another city or even a criminal hoping for lenient punishment, the supplicant would wrap their arms about the king's legs and invoke Zeus Soter, or "saviour." The mortal king then drew his divine power and subsequently exalted position in society from the fact that Zeus Basileus, "the king," resided within him. When the king led his army out to battle, Zeus Promachos, loosely translated as "pro-war," stood by his side. These aspects of Zeus are but a few that he had, each one both a god and a part of a god simultaneously.

In order to understand this, it is necessary to imagine the gods as divine powers who represent cosmic aspects of the universe that are always present and always in conflict. Vernant gave the example of the ancient Greeks connecting Zeus with the sky while, at the same time, making a distinction between two areas of sky. For the ancient Greeks, the sky was divided into the "constantly luminous" and brilliantly incorruptible Aither, and the Aer, which is "the zone of atmospheric phenomena whose unpredictable violence is of the first importance in the life of men since it is the source of the winds, clouds, and beneficial rain, and also of destructive storms."[31] Understanding this duplicity in relation to Zeus makes it easier to understand why he would start the greatest war hitherto experienced simply because he wanted to see the heroes reach their potential.

Each god had a specific form of knowledge and power, and the rivalry and conflict between them represents the cosmos as the ancient Greeks witnessed it. Undoubtedly, the ancient Greeks enjoyed the stories of Zeus and Hera bickering, but they also "saw the divine cosmos torn by tensions, contradictions and conflicts of prerogatives and power."[32] Nevertheless, these confusing tensions all took place beneath Zeus's divine cosmic law of unity, ensuring the return to Chaos would never take place.

The role of the gods in society was both demonstrative and active. In terms of being demonstrative, the gods battled to create the immovable and natural, yet heavenly hierarchy that was recreated amongst mortals. Zeus was the head of the pantheon as a king was the head of a city and a father the head of a household. There was a strict hierarchy that needed to be implemented in order for the Polis (i.e. city-state) to function. This hierarchy had the gods (Theoi) at the top, the Heroes (and Daimones) below them, the "Blessed Dead" spirits below the Heroes, and the living mortals at the bottom of the ladder. Furthermore, recalling the distance between the reader of the story of Troy (which only increased after the Classical Philosophers) and the heroes they read about, could help the modern reader distinguish between the story and their public or private religious thoughts.

The active aspect of the gods in social religion involved the roles they played in everyday religious life. Religion served to integrate aspects of the individual into society. These "powers" — love, war, justice, joy — reside in every person and in all aspects of society, and lacking one

---

[31] ibid.
[32] ibid.

or more of these powers was considered perilous. For instance, Aphrodite punished Menelaus for neglecting to dedicate the gift he promised to her. This is at once an example of the fickleness of the "Aphrodite Power," as well as a socio-cultural warning to anybody neglecting that aspect of their personality. "[The gods' epithets] make it possible to integrate the human individual into various social groups, each with its own ordered way of functioning and its own hierarchy; and to integrate these social groups, in their turn, into the order of nature which is then made a part of the divine order."[33]

Aspects of the gods as powers appeared in every walk of life, particularly in politics. For a woman who was legislatively barred from taking part in politics, there were religious functions that brought individuals out of the *polis* and into nature. These functions focused on a more "personal religion," such as the Bacchic rites and the Eleusinian Mysteries.

The cosmic hierarchy is made up of esoteric powers that affect and integrate into the same structure that is imitated and enacted on earth. The ancient Greek theological cycle is best described in Vernant's own words: "The Greeks knew perfectly well that a king was not a force of nature and that a force of nature was not the same as a deity. Nevertheless, they saw them as linked, interdependent, as different aspects of a single divine power."

The gods' roles in the Trojan War are obviously vital to the story, and the popularity of the *Iliad* for nearly 3,000 years. Although it was certainly not the last episode in the Heroic Age, the roles and personalities of the gods did not change much after this period. Indeed, by the Classical era, thinkers such as Plato and Aristotle began to disregard what was said about the gods in the *Iliad* and the *Odyssey* (with its story of Aphrodite and Ares cuckolding poor Hephaestus) as almost sacrilegious. These events are disregarded simply as fantasy and methods of narration, and by the time of Virgil, they were put to use again in the *Aeneid*, which aimed to worship Emperor Augustus and serve as propaganda.

Ultimately, the essence of the story's enduring popularity is the simple fact that the episodes leading up to and including the sack of Troy are episodes in an excellent, yet greater, story. The sum is greater than its parts, all of which incorporate themes that have survived centuries and will no doubt survive many more to come.

Online Resources

Other books about ancient history by Charles River Editors

Other books about ancient Greece by Charles River Editors

Other books about the Trojan War on Amazon

---

[33] ibid.

Further Reading

Apollodorus *Biblioteca* with an English Translation by Sir James George Frazer, F.B.A., F.R.S. in 2 Volumes. Cambridge, MA, Harvard University Press; London, William Heinemann Ltd. (1921).

Ashliman, L., *A Guide to Folktales in the English Language: Based on the Aarne-Thompson Classification System* Greenwood (1987).

Fontenrose, J., Python: A Study of Delphic Myth and Its Origins (1959).

Grimm, J; Grimm, W; Tatar, M; Byatt, A.S., *The Annotated Brothers Grimm: The Bicentennial Edition: Bicentennial Edition, Expanded and Updated,* W. W. Norton & Company , (2012).

Herodotus, *Histories* with an English translation by A. D. Godley. Cambridge. Harvard University Press. (1920).

Kirk, G. S., *Myth: Its Meaning And Function In Ancient And Other Cultures* University of California Press (1996).

Pausanias, *Description of Greece* with an English Translation by W.H.S. Jones, Litt.D., and H.A. Ormerod, M.A., in 4 Volumes. Cambridge, MA, Harvard University Press (1918).

Plutarch, *Moralia* with an English Translation by. Frank Cole Babbitt. Cambridge, MA. Harvard University Press (1936).

Propp, Vladimir., Morphology of the Folk Tale. University of Austin Texas (1968).

Statius, *Achilleid* Translated by Mozley, J H. Loeb Classical Library Cambridge, MA, Harvard University Press (1928).

Thucydides, *The Peloponnesian War* London, J. M. Dent; New York, E. P. Dutton. (1910).

Vernant, J. P., *Myth and Society in Ancient Greece* Zone Books (1996).

Free Books by Charles River Editors

We have brand new titles available for free most days of the week. To see which of our titles are currently free, click on this link.

Discounted Books by Charles River Editors

We have titles at a discount price of just 99 cents everyday. To see which of our titles are currently 99 cents, click on this link.

Made in the USA
Columbia, SC
03 June 2018